For Valerie —

The Earth Is Not Flat

As ever, with
pleasure and warm
regards —

Kate

The Earth Is Not Flat

poems by

Katharine Coles

Red Hen Press | *Pasadena, CA*

Book design and layout by Skyler Schulze

Library of Congress Cataloging-in-Publication Data

Coles, Katharine.
 [Poems. Selections]
 The earth is not flat : poems / by Katharine Coles.—First edition.
   pages cm
 Includes bibliographical references.
 ISBN 978-1-59709-710-9
 I. Title.
 PS3553.O47455E27 2013
 811'.54—dc23
                    2012044237

The Los Angeles County Arts Commission, the Los Angeles Department of Cultural
Affairs, the Dwight Stuart Youth Fund, the City of Pasadena Cultural Affairs Division,
and Sony Pictures Entertainment partially support Red Hen Press. This publication was
supported in part by an award from the National Endowment for the Arts.

First Edition
Published by Red Hen Press
www.redhen.org

Acknowledgments

I gratefully acknowledge the following journals in which poems from this collection first appeared:

1010, "Self-Portrait in Hiding"; *Ascent*, "Charismatic Diatoms," "Problems of Description in the Language of Discovery," "Walking the Glacier"; *Axon*, "Abandon," "Fixing Antarctica," "In the End," "Self-Portrait as Erasure," "Self-Portrait in Glass," "To Alice, the Beast Appears"; *Bacon Review*, "Inadvertent Self-Portrait," "Looking South," "Two Kinds of People"; *Connotation Press*, "Antimanifesto"; *Crazy Horse*, "Mirage," "Not Just Having the Feeling"; *Grist*, "Cognito," "Glass House," "Landscape Without Bicycle"; *Image*, "Faith," "Habits of Invention"; *Literary Bohemian*, "Dog Years"; *Poetry*, "Tempo for a Winged Instrument"; *Rhino*, "Exit Interview"; *Route 7 Review*, "Passage," "Proposal"; *Seneca Review*, "Use /   / in a Sentence"; *Virginia Quarterly Review*, "Rumors of Topography," "Sailing to Antarctica," "Tattoo," "Terra Lab," "The Human Mind Did Not Create the Ice"; *Shadowbox*, "May Day"; and *Web Conjunctions*, "Cento from Various Non-Poetic Sources," "Dogs of Ice," "Here Be Monsters."

As Auden says, "No one exists alone." I have received help and support from so many others, including but not limited to the editors of the journals listed above, that I can't possibly list everyone by name, though it might seem to readers that I must have. So:

"Problems of Description in the Language of Discovery" was published in a fine, letterpress artist's book by the Red Butte Press in 2012. The design team comprised Press Director Marnie Powers-Torrey, designer David Wolke, artist Mary Toscano, and book artists Emily Tipps and Becky Thomas.

"Clock Erasure" was set with three other of my poems for soprano by composer Steven Roens as a part of a sequence, "Elegies," commissioned by the Eschler Music Foundation and premiered in Boston in April 2012.

"Here Be Monsters," "Landscape With Fire," and "On Landscape" were part of an installation by visual artist Maureen O'Hara Ure, with whom I have collaborated for over twenty years.

"Landscape with Fire" appeared on the Antelope Valley's Sagebrush Café coffee cups as part of Nicelle Davis's "Stick With Me Poetry Project."

This material is based upon work supported by the National Science Foundation under Grant No. 0840023. Any opinions, findings, and conclusions or recommendations expressed in this material are those of the author(s) and do not necessarily reflect the views of the National Science Foundation. I extend my most grateful thanks to the NSF and its Antarctic Artists and Writers Program; to Peter West, Bob Farrell, and other administrators of that program, and especially to Tracy Baldwin, who warned me in advance that none of the NSF-issued clothing would fit me and I'd better buy my own; and to the scientists and colleagues at Palmer Station who were incomparably generous and giving with their time and intelligence, many of whom appear by name in these poems and the notes to the poems. Thanks also to Charles Hood, whose research and work have buoyed and enlightened me; to my husband, Chris Johnson, who may forgive me yet and who led me to the title for this collection; to Melanie Rae Thon for her generous and brilliant readings of these poems and, even more, for her generous and brilliant love; and not least to Kate Gale and Mark Cull of Red Hen Press for their support of this project and others and also for their deep and abiding wisdom, friendship, and hospitality.

Contents

III. Rumors of Topography

The Earth Is Not Flat

I. Reckless

Self-Portrait in Hiding

If you wanted to be first
You live in the wrong time. Through

An old lens: the same ice
Grinding over itself, turning up
Blue, pink, twilight. Everything

Frozen in motion. How long
Does it take light to evaporate

Completely? Longer for you
Falling like sleep, but not
Exactly. Without shadow, the ice

Stretches smooth before your boots
Though it opens crevasses

Everywhere to get you down
Cold. Tell me
You will never be

So awake, without shadow
Invisibly yourself.

Stare at the Sun

Our glass concentrates sunlight
1000 times. The sidewalk's image

Takes in everything the light passes
Through—a bare trellis,

Tracery of limbs
Exposed. Where I'm going

Only clouds cast
Shadows from above. Oh, and birds

Fleeting. The weathervane. The eye's
Lens concentrates the sun

2500 times, focusing it
Back onto the retina. Which

For a moment sees everything
Whole, the shape of a leaf opening then

Beaming so bright before it
Dazzles, goes up in smoke.

Proposal

1. To pore over maps for months in advance. The ones I prefer, centuries out of date, know nothing useful.

2. To take notes on the maps' imaginative fillips, monsters stretching out along their borders waiting to charm.

3. To learn the names of charted harbors and islands and their relative locations from a birds-eye view though I am not a bird, as if sitting at my kitchen table with paper spread before me will have been the same as rising and falling on wind or water, caught between cold sky and drowning.

4. To close my eyes here at my table and imagine cold sky, drowning, wings that carry a body between. My imagination, like my observation, relies on inaccuracy, approximation, desire.

5. To read journals and letters and notebooks by those who have gone before. I will learn what it might have felt like to be the first, to cross ice on foot pulling a sledge, ride the sea's extravagant curl in a small boat using my shirt as a sail, butcher and eat my dogs, which I may or may not have learned to love for something more than usefulness.

6. I promise to accept I will never be first and have little chance of doing half those other things either. I will never be an engineer or learn how to rig useful devices from what I carry in my handbag—wire and tape, a battery, stray parts from Radio Shack. Still, I will commit myself to practical details, attend to sleeping arrangements and rigging and keeping small flames alive.

7. To prove I am worthy, I will let machines read my heart and run until my breath fails or the monitor gets tired of me, whichever comes first. I will let the vials have as much blood as they can hold.

8. I will fill out forms and acquire hats and gloves and waterproof trousers.

9. When I get there at last, someone will look over my supplies clucking his tongue. Someone will provide pencils and a notebook that takes the lead even when wet, the pages of which won't be erased by weather or doubt. Someone—maybe you?—will issue canvas overalls, second-hand long johns, flannel shirts, a suit to keep me afloat if I go overboard. From these, I will learn how small I really am, even by human scale, and that my shirt will never fly. I will imagine the other scales a body might live on, extra-extra-extra-large and also so minute I will never see them. I will belt the pants and roll my cuffs to ankle and wrist.

10. From within my smallness within the future, I will study land and water as they lie or shift on a given day, where the glacier hides its crevasses, which islands hold emergency caches and how to pitch the tents and light the stoves those caches contain, even in a gale.

11. I will learn not to call a smart breeze a gale. I will learn to fix an outboard motor and how to use it to spin a Zodiac backward in giddy pirouette. I will steer through brash ice and floes, will mount the swell and ride it down. I will learn the physics of all of this.

12. No matter where I am, I will stay ahead of myself, becoming a hitchhiker, riding every boat and iceberg that stops for me.

13. I will cross the line on the map. I will prove the fanciful creatures and invent new ones. If I can get close enough I will feed them, placing my palm under their noses, feeling the warm graze of breath then teeth as they lip my tender morsels into their mouths. Doing so will violate treaties among nations, among worlds.

14. Of course, I promise to obey all treaties.

15. I propose to save myself. To make lists. To carry dry socks at all times.

16. I will get close enough. To what I can't yet say. Already, I'm full of glee.

17. At some point, I promise, I will begin.

FAITH

I understand the problem. You make
A metaphor to try to heal

Something. At its heart is a wound

You put there. Write
A postcard, send it off—now

Believe it will arrive

A whole planet away,
A lifetime, into another's hands. Try

Not thinking what might go wrong.

Reckless

1.

Once certain issues are addressed, a question remains: Why would you?

Fill in the blank.

Maybe the answers are short and simple: I wouldn't, or Why not, or I don't know.

Maybe you want to feel all the places your heart can make itself known inside your body—a pulse, a flutter, an unexpected empty space you are tempted to walk into.

If so, maybe your body too is a landscape constructed of displacement and mirage, pain generated one place but felt in another. So many false positives, or lost ones.

Think of all the things you mean when you say "heart."

Eating a heart is not the same as eating your heart out.

2.

Consider, then, what it would mean to say you do or don't have reck. Whether it is something you can set aside or you must be born without. Whether it can be weighed and measured.

Maybe your body is also made of light and water, air and dust, ice and an anxiety you want to probe with your fingers. Maybe it is everything you imagine.

Is it there?

3.

This is a train wreck, I say, even when there is no train in sight.

4.

For example, a Belgian artist living in Mexico has many ways to begin. Sometimes he starts a rumor; sometimes he runs after tornadoes, looking to fly. He will slam to earth for the sake of an idea or maybe a feeling, for the sake not of sweeping over an open field but of imagining he might be swept into the great next time.

Watching the video, you will want to go with him or not. You will be inside or outside the frame, breathing or breathless, mover or voyeur. You will be struck.

Many things can bring you down.

This might happen over and over. You might become the picture of diligence.

There might be a lack of observation or care. A reckoning. Perhaps recognition will dawn or never set, merely enter a long twilight.

5.

Take heed: I have no idea who you are. If I whisper to you, believe

I might try to turn you, get you to take a spin.

Provide, provide.

TWO KINDS OF PEOPLE

Those who love the wind, and. Those
Who believe in words. Or who believe

In time as if an instant were something
Anyone could measure, who believe anything

Can be divided into two. Or three. And.
Those who leave all the lights

Blazing the darkest night of the year; who sit
Alone under one lamp reading, waiting

For the eclipse even if the moon does
Take all damned night and the sun

Never sets; who fly
As far as they must to find—

Who may, who knows, be the same
People. Our friend Torsten says there are

Those who dream of climbing a ladder
Down any hole in the ice, who would, waving

Hats overhead, fling themselves into
Volcano or blizzard, into the sea's

Lowest trough and over the next crest, and those
Like Deb who would say, I support you

But what, are you crazy? Who
Are you? Which am I? One then

The other takes two hearts in hand
And sails into almost any

Earthly end, then returns to solid
Ground rocking, each other's arms.

Self-Portrait is Not to Scale

Who do I talk to here? Myself
And you, who may be the same. The inner life

Diminishes, when the outer vastly
Insists upon itself. Or not. Just

Being, the way my friend tells me to,
Is better than I am. It all is.

Drake Passage

The whole ocean funnels through east to west, building upon itself.

Because there is nothing to stop it, we learn to roll along the ship's hallways, both hands on the rails, and up and down

Stairs falling underfoot or scaling to meet us, and so not to think about the sea's roughed-over surface opening dark and cold beneath

Or to think what bears us aloft, giving and giving, that could take us whole.

Dog Years

When I'm home, she follows me floor to floor
Without complaint, lugging fifteen year-old bones,
Settling once she knows again where we are.
Now I'm gone, she lies by the front door

Watching through the glass for my car.
I have never seen this—but I know when
I open the door at last, she'll be there.
My husband recounts by satellite phone the hours

She lay there today, rising only to make sure
I hadn't sneaked back in while she was asleep
Or to watch him fill her bowl, then not eat.
Every minute you're gone feels like forever,

He says, his voice travelling all the way
To space and back before it reaches me.

Sailing to Antarctica

The problem is the voices

I can't get out of my head. On the bridge, the captain's playing
"Break On Through"; he's been

Playing "Stormy Weather." Go ahead, Google *World's*

Roughest Crossing. Google
Shipwreck, and *Lost at Sea*. Meanwhile, the ship

Is tearing itself

Apart, isn't it, beam by steel beam; the ship is gnawing its own liver
And the sea is eating

Its heart out and wants me to sashay right on by and take

A look. Lean over
The rail, little one, lean a little farther. The problem is the voices. Sea,

Sea, you're all foam

Vanishing, cry of shearwater and albatross wing knitting
You to sky; you are height

And depth and open mouth, and I am barely a morsel. Sea, I can't get out

Of my head, or is it you're
What I can't get my poor head around, what I don't know how to measure—

A 20-foot sea, a 30-foot sea. Not a falling so much as a

Career, a sinking
So much as a gulp. Measure from where the surface would be

If I could find it, if

The idea of surface hadn't become a moving target I plummet
Past into the trough and know

No better on the ride back up into yippee, though on the wave's crest

Three days out
I would swear I can see South America. This is the best

Thing ever, clinging

To the rail watching another wave crash all the way over the bow, over
The captain high

In his bridge, the captain who will carry us through with his instruments

And playlist and steel-hulled
Gut, though he says everyone has a threshold, even him. Chris and Jenny,

Most of the passengers

Green in their berths along with half the crew. And me, I am used
To the world appearing

To wish me well. All those summer weeks spent reading in the Jeep

While Dad careened us down
The roughest roads he could find, Mom hanging from some near

Cliff face by

Rope rigging. Isn't a mountain a wave moving slow? I am
Used to the best

Kind of luck and a stomach that can ride out anything, even

The swell
Of my own hubris. All day I stand on deck with the birds

And spray, birds

That can sail across oceans without moving their wings. Wherever
I look, infinity's blue

And grey, and I say *Okay already, give me all you've got.*

JOB

He, not I. *Waters   hid.*
Beleaguered, *hoary*, everything

Leagued against. *Out of*
                    Heaven

Gendered. A woman
May be. *Whose womb*. Ship

Bellying. I believe
I'm safe. *Hid   a stone*. Ship

Dropping, rising
With a stone

Thirty feet at once. *Frost*
Of Heaven I know

No hardship. *Frozen*
                    Face

Of the deep   out of whose he
And I stranded.

Beginning with an erasure of verses quoted by Shackleton

Ship Songs

Day and night small beings die behind the walls,
Resurrect back into voice. It is

No singular grief or song, that chirrup

Winding its strangled hiccup down then
Starting up again. The strong man hammers

Pipes, lost in his clamor. The sailor

Sighs with every dip and roll, remembering
The sea always drops out from under

What he's lost.

Here Be Monsters

We could fall off one
Edge or another. Water

Roils and troubles as if it would

Throw itself over, and glacier
Meets sea by pushing into

Erosion's demand and response. Fissure

Could swallow a body whole
Then close on itself, sucking

Its tongue. Feel

The earth's end old maps
Elaborate with what's unknown

But fully imagined, voracious

Tooth and claw
White to the bone. Just beyond

The horizon, right over

There is the trouble
Trying to picture our progress

Straight and flat. It doesn't matter

If we finish on water
Or land, on ice or the deck of a ship

Taking flight. At the wave's top

The body hangs weightless
In its turn. It doesn't matter

As soon as we arrive at any point

We're headed out the other side,
A place beyond which

There is no beyond except

In the mind, which is
It turns out the body after all

Where we live, whole-

Hearted. Where surface will not hold
We must shatter.

II. Cold Heart

Cold Heart

When we meet, he says, Oh,
You have such warm hands.

Nobody has ever said
This to me before.

How does he know me
So quickly and so well?

Cognito

The young men have names like PQ and DeValle, Nandi and Rex, C-Note, the Beaver. One introduces himself as Logistics and shakes my hand.

They sport dark full beards and stocking caps, plaid flannel shirts, government-issued Carhartts.

The flannel shirts all look the same to me.

One of them lent me a *National Geographic* my first day here. I looked up at ice then down at pictures of ice.

At breakfast I sit down across from someone and pass the salt. Together, we work the crossword, me reading upside-down until someone comes by and names him. Is he the one who lent me the magazine? Red in the beard, hazel eyes, not too tall.

Then comes the moustache party. The young men shave their beards, revealing chilly-looking chins, frighteningly individual, leaving identical dark sieves on their upper lips.

Except the one who carves out whimsical mutton chops: Rex.

Two days later, they shave the moustaches too, and the sideburns. Their faces, naked, look surprised at themselves.

In time, I learn DeVal and Rex are also nicknames. All the young men have
at least two names in use, sometimes three. Nandi is short for the given name,
Nandoor.

When I was getting ready, I kept getting emails saying I wasn't PQ. I had no
idea what that meant. I submitted this form, then that one—vaccinations,
checked-off pages of blood values, results of treadmill test and ECG and mam-
mogram. Finally, I received an email saying, You are now Physically Qualified.

About the young man called PQ, I may have made assumptions. Would it help
me to know what is behind the letters?

Paul, Peter, Pierrot?

Quest, Quarrel, Quarry, Quisling?

Quantum, Quintessence, Quail, Quad, Quince?

Not Just Having the Feeling

1. But being able to name it, at least the features it shares with some other feeling you already know.

2. Like the virus you've never seen before, backlit against the microscope's slide: find a familiar bump or trail of hairs, likeness to hook it to, to draw it from the netherworld, where everything lives until it has a name, into this world.

3. Otherwise, the feeling, the virus, that bird flying not through air but through water, is the ghost of something.

4. The woman from the cruise ship says, I have no words for this place. None of the superlatives will do.

5. Out on the water, I can hardly tell one island from the other, there are so many to learn, or them from the point where my tiny home perches—until I say there's the glacier, and am replaced.

6. From there, I know Cormorant, Old Palmer, Jacobs. This one has birds, that one topography, and an iceberg we call Mark Wahlberg lets the wind take him where it will.

7. Here, on station, the sky fills the whole window, as does the ocean, and there is nothing we can do about it.

8. The window gives a limit.

9. Outside on the walkway, a sheathbill dawdles, looking like Winston Churchill. The glacier

10. Cycles through its moods, this one blue.

The Human Mind Did Not Create the Ice

Nor its manifold mirages, billows and mountains
And mislaid islands shifting by the minute, which nonetheless

Do exist—as image, not as body
The way the ice is body, until it melts. Mathematics

Did not create refraction, only how we account for it,
Its sly angles and inferences and wild confabulations,

Its continuous slips of the tongue. Mathematics: did it
Exist before we made it? John Burgess said,

"As far as I'm concerned, the stars can't be
Socially constructed." Stars mean stars

Are reconstructed, twinkling
Created by distortion, light traveling through

Vast improbabilities, through the lenses of our telescopes
Upturned and of our eyes, to be cast away at last upon

The retinas of eye then brain. Is it a violence, this
Intrusion? Clusters of cells shuttling the image

Deep, all the way to the eye we always felt
Inside. Now, we know it's not only there

But real, looking inward as we do with scanners
And microscopes, instruments we assembled just for this.

CHARISMATIC DIATOMS

It could be a map of the sky—
This slide we bend to while the real thing
Stretches its endless daylit self above—blazing

With ray-shot heads explosive
As novas, charismatic as any heavenly body
Charted in singular dimensions, traceries

Laid still for the eye, laid out in segments
And floral clusters, outlining swords
And girdles fit for Amazon waists, bottles

Brimming gold, fragile parachutes blowing open
And waiting to be named, to be assigned
That kind of meaning. As if

A name made any difference. It could be
A map of the future then, on which signs loom
To be read across time, through which

Each season will trail stories we must enact,
Flashing urgent as comets' tails, ushering in
Another brilliant idea before which

We are helpless. Fated, dazzled, all this bright-
Long day, I gazed at the horizon,
Receding distance made of stone, water,

Vivid ice and sky. Light and wind burned
My eyes: nothing I could see
Turning to sting and ache, as if

A good scouring could open me. Beneath us,
The sea took long breaths, coming out
Of its dark age into summer's

Star-struck bloom. Now, at the microscope,
How deep into time do you think we might see?
Backward, forward. Same

Old romancers, leaning over intricate
Puzzles, teasing meaning from figures
Flying aloof under steady, considering lights.

Terra Lab

We are not allowed to take photographs.
Not allowed to tell you certain things
Or which things those are. The screens

Display results if you know how to read
Blues and yellows spiking and shading, showing

The eye how much noise there is
At each frequency. This place is clean,
Electromagnetically speaking. We can hear

Lightning strike anywhere in the world, shifted
Electrons whistling and cracking, diving

Back to earth, the wind playing
Its parts. If a nuclear bomb goes off
The instrument will notice. It moves its flibberty-

Bits faster than sound. This I believe
I'm allowed to tell you. I'm not allowed

To show you how it's done. Above us
The ozone layer thickens and thins, and somebody
Knows that too. A machine collects air

And turns it into numbers; someone plays
The guitar leaning in the corner. Me, I can't

Stop listening to the weather. Picture
Disturbance, and with it a sky you knew gone
Static, pin-pricked, too dark.

Self-Portrait in Glass

Between liquid and crystal, I am
Holding firm, trying to see through

Myself. I could magnify what is past me
Or flip and turn an ice-locked continent

Crossed with gorges and fissures to
A leaf just coming out. That kind of day,

Blue one minute with sun on my face
And the next full of flakes stinging

My cheeks to water. In such a moment, neither
One thing nor the other, what would I know?

He Completes Me

Maybe better than nothing, these
Flickering ghosts appearing late

At night when the bandwidth's open. At least
We can see each other, he says, but like

Our voices over the sat phone, our faces travel
Space and through everything

Space contains: winds and quirks and flurries,
Dust and ice shattering. Delayed,

Thwarted even before it leaves
My own screen, my face goes yellow,

Misshapen—narrowed beyond any waning
The mirror shows. And his, dismantled, arrives

In bits and pieces: intact eyebrow, mouth moving
Only one lip, eyes and nose broken, so star-

Crossed even the machine can't
Translate or put them back together.

Inadvertent Self-Portrait

The inadvertent self begins in the You, which
A therapist might call terminal. It may or may not be

Worth listening to. Out here, in
The ongoing vast now, it seems even

Smaller than usual, even more subject
To expansion and persuasion. Its neural circuitry

Applies itself continuously, no matter
How cold it is or how much light

Hurts the eyes and then, burrowing in
Deep, the brain. Tap, tap, tap goes the light

Except when it impresses itself, as everything
Does, in waves. Though it may not be aware,

The inadvertent self undergoes constant
Remodeling, entering every second

A new relation, in which revelation or
Even simple insight never is given, however

We try not to lose it. All its organ systems
Excite, even those it never considers. It shuffles

And sorts. It doesn't panic yet. The inadvertent self
Keeps a stiff upper lip, has backbone, confines

Itself to ordinary angst, however uniquely
Specific it feels. It is a moving target.

Directional

An old joke: so many signs
Pointing from the middle of nowhere

Everywhere anyone calls home,
Always north, and the iron whale,

Also hammered by hand, in theory
Meant to swivel at any breath but pointed

Northeast, no matter
The wind's direction, for which

We watch the flags. Here,
We make what we make

Do with. Southwesterlies
Fix our attention, bearing

Themselves across ocean so open
It won't slow any weather, but builds

Mass and force, wave
Upon wave piling our way.

Landscape with Fire

Eyes open and burning. Heart
A furnace blowing red. In all this

White and grey and blue—cloud
And glacier, sea and sky, shag

Winging around the shag's eye—
One warm thing. What I feel

Isn't always true. Here, I'm not
The only thing that moves.

MUSIC OF THE SPHERES

After Stellar Axis by Lita Albuquerque

Bring to this particular field constant

Motion, stars we never see now
Even night shines. Turn them on

Earth's axis as the universe does, but not

Exactly. Brilliant beyond. Watch them
Warble as they move—surface, like

Everything, their playground. Turn

Again, just see how they go and listen
Why don't you until some high note

Spirals out, a note you can name

If you let yourself be moved. So much
We have seen before is already gone

Or was never there and still

Vanished. I've often dreamed white earth
That cannot be smoothed down, blue orb

Spinning, I hear, behind blue eye.

Penguin and Human

Which report would you believe,
Sitting in your parlor back in London
In, say, 1550: the new world sighting

Of the unicorn you've seen in paintings
And read about in poems, now at last
Witnessed; or that of these creatures

Waddling over rocks and icebergs, waving
Useless wings? Invented by some
Disreputable tar, drunk

Or snow-blind. There, on land, is where
They seem most like us, distracted
And inept, or would if they paid

Attention to our intrusions. They don't
Recognize us, busy with this
Pebble or that, with an egg then a chick,

With the enormous brown skuas waiting
Right over there for a look at something
Delectable. They fail to notice. Then one

Takes to the water and takes
Our breath—flight stitching wave to sky
First going by, then coming round

Again—flirting with our boat's
Deep idle purr; and each of us, turning
Head to follow, saying, Oh.

SELF-PORTRAIT WITH ELEPHANT SEAL

Only the seal can know what she means,
Calling and calling from no leg to stand on
To the other seals, the water

Lapping her tail. Itchy all over
But able to reach and scratch with tiny flippers
A few-inch range, graceless here on land

Underwater she is sleek as a fish
And full of her own power. Anyway,
Who am I to talk? In my yellow rubber

Boating overalls and too-big boots
I'm just another clumsy mammal
Out of its element. Together

We share this moment in the sun, which is
Doorway, hinge, aperture to what
Neither of us will say.

Tempo for a Winged Instrument

Full of light and music, the beating air.

Light like a bird, Calvino says, not a feather.

Over the water the shags come in to land

All wings, uh-ohing over the cliffs.

Rock, their nests, and bare the rookeries.

Blue eye, blue eye, the wind plays fast and sharp.

They lift and ride and do not pick their fights.

Oh, blue sky, blue day. Heart

Of muscle, thrumming down, and swift.

Cento from Various Non-Poetic Sources

A signal of danger has arrived in consciousness.
It is a metaphysically pointed arrangement.

The clarity of light is an astronomer's dream,

Mostly random, a fluke of the heart. Every scale
And spiny fin is neatly articulated. But that is not all:

A single big bird plummets straight down from the sky.

The question is not what you look at, but what you see.
The eye is not innocent, it is already committed.

Peacock Dolphin

Snatched glimpse from the dry-docked Zodiac, Terrible
Storm: elusive, spreading its caprice of tail,
Eyes trembling on blue-green stalks
Then slapping shut. It arches into the water,

Folding wings to dorsal slicing the waves,
Snapping them into a sail to pull the wind.
I can only follow as it glances between
The swells and chunks of brash ice and—

Palm trees? So habited, my mind won't
Stoop to dream the creature I'm looking for,
Who will eat from my hand, close and open
Itself at my command, go anywhere

I will. Why should it? My siren sings, then dives.
It draws me down. Nothing else can live.

To Alice, the Beast Appears

Say a creature glows in the dark, body
And soul afloat on a sea

So southern you have to pass through
An underworld to get

Where it's never dark. You've dreamt
This creature's spine and head and extravagant

Tail lifted from the water so elegantly
It must be curious, preening, still

As life. You know
It's apocryphal. You take one photo

After another. Carved ice, blue
Water you must jump into, though

You'll take years to get your nerve,
A day to stop chattering. I dreamed

The creature. Alice pointed it out
In this world, in which its push-

Me pull-you shape keeps
Changing. So pure, we could

Chisel chunks off to chill
Our drinks. Instead, we leave it to sail wind

And tide toward its necessary
Vanishing. Ice-blind, we see right through it.

No Wonder

                    even penguins
Are afraid of the dark, little

Adelies escaping fast

As they can into summer
Wherever it is. North,

South. Invent something

Probable. Think how
They feel, swimming

Just ahead of the night,

Which, someday, even they
Will not be able to outrun.

MIRAGE

I don't need to see
What is real. Iridium-pure, corrupted
Only by light. So *icebergs hang*

Upside-down. I need to see
What he sees. *From the mast-head*
false alarms. Oh,

Unreality. I'm unalarmed. *In the sky,*
The land appears. Cloudbanks masquerade. What
On earth? I have never

Been able to tell one thing
From another. *Icebergs thrown into view*
Worst of all. Why start now? Say

Sun shining at an angle might be
North Dakota. *On a field of smooth snow* this
Midnight here looks like that

High noon and I never once
Missed it. *Ice-cliffs*
Below the horizon I have never seen

So far. *The appearance*
Of open water. Absence of shadows. In light
We go to sleep. *The inland ice*

Appeared. Wake to
Dazzling whiteness, shadows
Dim blue or faint. What he says

(Deceptive, distant, barrier) I might
Have said. *Outside*
Our range of vision under

This sun *something*
Masquerades. Everything new. *The face*
Curiously human.

Beginning with an erasure from Shackleton

ALL DAY LONG THE GLACIER SINGS

With as many voices as throats
Whale song, birdsong, human,

Tea-kettle, trolley, type-writer. The glacier
Moans like any sotted lover,

Misplays pipes in its own parade;
It rumbles its stomach and chafes

Its legs together and clatters high
Heels across the pavement, refusing

Key or rhythm, slipping between
Notes to find itself. Today, the glacier

Could tell us everything, if we
Would listen. We try,

Cocking our heads, not knowing
What or how to answer.

WALKING THE GLACIER

Even here, breaking surface
One hard step at a time, so much of what I do

Is plodding along, forgetting it's easy
To keep sounding myself. Do I

Forget what I'm saying? Distracted,
My brain mutters something about

An old injury it hangs onto, not even
Meant for me. I hear there's training

For this too. Meanwhile, I find myself
Surprised to be unzipping under

Such a wind, how hard my body becomes
To carry. They let me

Come up all alone, the whole
Place to myself. Not afraid it seems

To lose me. Sink, flail and pull back
Out, sink again. The view,

Will it dazzle? I can't see the edge
Where ice bears itself away

Continually, just under my feet
The raft that carries me over invisibly

Splitting. If I forget myself, I could
Become spectacular. Could throw

Myself, whole hearted, into something
Or off. Stop. Look. Blaze

And shadow. So blue
My stars falling away.

BARE-KNUCKLED SELF-PORTRAIT

If I were always present, maybe
I would know where I'd put

My gloves, without which
I can go nowhere. Meanwhile

The sun kindly shines
Me into bodied light.

LIFE: STUDIES IN FRAGMENTS

What made you, intimate
connection,
                    somewhat

 human? The world seems
first hand. Peekaboo holes, precise

and technical, pin things
down. Almost

byproduct: a new species,
garrulous eggs, verse

with a vestigial
knack for meandering. Real things

chased by a tiger have
a way of falling

down, a kind of joy. Irritated
reader, whimsical

old man in bed, dismiss
appropriation—the golden

monkey a figment
in the form of flame,
            of imagination.

A much-rearranged erasure from "Life Studies"
by Richard Coniff, NYT, February 2011

ANTIMANIFESTO

No woman's poem diminishes me.
The men's poems I'll take

One at a time. No poem ever took the space
Meant for another poem. No poem ever

Forced me to listen. There's no theory
I wouldn't surrender for a line, no line

I wouldn't cast out for a nibble. I've never
Believed in art or its purity. I would believe

If believing wrote a poem. What good
Would it do me to insist? The world is

Its own machine. The world turns
And turns again, and then the world decides.

Use / / in a Sentence

1. On warm mornings the bay is choked with / /.

2. *Saturated* *floating* *under heavy snowfall*

3. maybe the / / is already a poem.

4. A / / is like an

5. / / only smaller.

6. How many names for / / can you come up with?

7. Did / / exist before its name?

8. Men in fur, putting the / / into words.

9. Men with / /-bitten fingers,

10. with / / in their beards.

11. Beyond definition, *the wreckage of other forms.*

12. Beyond measurement, beyond *accumulation.*

13. I keep saying "gash" when I mean / /.

14. I am lying on the shelf *almost awash.*

15. I am lying down *with raised rims,* among

16. / / *formed from /* / *or the wreckage*

17. of / /. Sometimes I am and sometimes not *attached to a coast.*

18. In Italian, / / means *loose gravel* or *stone made,* perhaps and perhaps not *formed on a quiet surface or under agitated conditions.*

19. You won't learn anything useful from me. Tongue-tied, I don't know how to see

20. except that / / *protrudes up to 6.5 feet above sea level.*

21. In English here and now / / *can be categorized.*

a.	Floe	h.	Frazil	o.	Grease
b.	Old	i.	Brash	p.	Shelf
c.	Growler	j.	Cake	q.	Young
d.	Slush	k.	Floeberg	r.	Bergy Bits
e.	Pancake	l.	Nilas	s.	Tabular
f.	Rind	m.	Breccia	t.	Shuga
g.	Floebit	n.	Berg	u.	First-year

Beginning with an erasure from 21 Kinds of Ice *by Jennifer Bogo*

Problems of Description
in the Language of Discovery

With apologies to Ken Golden, mathematician

First, there's what you can do with a ruler
Only as precise as your hand that lays it
Alongside inclusions, ice crystals melting, surprisingly

       Similar in the abstract, whatever
       Their particular uniquenesses. When waves

Move the ship, your hand slips too. There's
What you can do in snow, what
In fire. What you can say about

       Any of it in numbers: say 5, operating
       Its own set of rules, magicked

Feathers fluttering from your sleeve. The change,
Sudden, where ice becomes not
Quite ice.
       Permeable.
             Excuse me:

       The mathematician, not the poet, deployed the word
       Magic, pulling the number

5 from which hat exactly? Unlike the poet, he's studied
Theories of percolation for decades, head
Bent between lamplight and numbers, considering

How everything gives way, at
What moment. Crunching the numbers

Again, knuckling them under. You might say he invents
Nothing, just observes, creates only
Models of what he's seen, if you haven't seen him

Flick his wrist. Tada! A moment ago
You stood on solid ground. Now

Look down and see water rising
Right over your boots. Ice
Underfoot seemed just that firm

Until you looked across to the horizon,
Bedazzled, and saw it heave. Measurable

Undulation. Keep watching the hand turning
You to distraction. What
With all we know about

Walking on water, why do we believe
Our eyes? In solid ground? -5°C, say. A brine

Fraction of 5%. If numbers appear from thin air, golden,
Anything gives way, ice or earth. I'm not here
To charm or conjure. I'm just watching,

As if, knowing what the numbers come to,
I might be able to tell you how they mean.

Dogs of Ice

What after all is necessary
Will we know it when it's in our hands

    we started with 52 dogs
    no abnormal strain

Helge, Mylius, Uroa   *in splendid condition*
Jimmy Pigg, Bones, Nobby   *hardly animal*

        the eyes the mirror a living soul
        joy sorrow gratitude scruples

Not forgetting ambition and desire
Not forgetting the ability to eat one's own

    Scott and his comrades were their own dogs
    to get the dogs to obey cost us a wet shirt

Odin, Thor, Lurvin
    ravenous dogs devoured
    whips lashings   ebonite points

    plaintive howls on the march
    I did not would not understand

Thinking about blinding light blue snow
A land by international accord empty of dogs

> *we had to chain Rex, Lasse*
> *in any case we had to reach 82° S*

I have pursued my own way my own desires
I did not would not understand

> *the whip lost its terrors*
> *crowded together heads out of the way*

> *the body did not matter*

There is the body I have held in my hands
Old now, blood moving under my palms

> *such endurance to equal*
What must be given up
leaning against my knees tail waving

He returned with eleven dogs
> *flogged home   grown fond*
> *the dog has not understood his master*

Who among us understands what drives us

> *the master has not understood his dog*

Under my hands blood and breath moving
Eyes a living soul her flesh beloved as any

    holiday humour ought to have prevailed

    when we cut him open
    his chest was one large abscess

I haven't even understood myself

Beginning with an erasure from Amundsen,
with a little Cherry-Garrard

ABANDON

On my screen, the hut is wood
Beams, light and shadow, a ship

Breasting rough land. Someone has just

Stepped out on deck, leaving me
A cup on the table, a book, a lantern

Waiting to swallow its flame

Alive. One chair knocked
Askew. What furniture I have

Rearranged for this. Because it is

Shot in black and white, I see
Its past—the scene, not the photos—as I am

Abandoned to the air of something

Kept artfully. From here no one
Can know if there are ghosts or how to live

Inside where I cultivate light

Or abroad in the vast emptiness, where I am
Never as wild or alone as I've felt. Mere

Suggestion in the arrangements: air

Bottled, trousers on the line still
Shaping a leg—you've heard all this—long

Gone. Here, dog harness

And biscuits, nail-studded wheel and oil
To feed the motor, gooseberries and currants and salt

Nobody ate, the dead

Penguin nobody salted and the books
Left to read or burn, spiked boots

And dog bones I'll never have to gnaw, men

And beasts also composed of light
And mind as durable as we come.

III. Rumors of Topography

Expedition Journal

On the way over—wake to snow.

On the way back—wake to rain.

In between, a stretch of sun

That seems it cannot end, under which

Mountains flow and ebb and the glacier

Changes its face, through which

Apparently endless blue

Tern and albatross present

Small differences to naming. We know,

The world insists. Then,

Before we know it, something else.

Landscape Without Bicycle

A two-wheeler wouldn't get you anywhere
Here, though one afternoon

An oceanographer ran the eighth-mile
Mud road from Bio to Terra Lab

And back one hundred times. Mired
Right up to its pedals, it wouldn't even

Cheer the place up. For that,
We have huge containers lined

Like lively teeth outside my window—
Yellow, red, blue, storing all

We throw away. A view of the dump
In primary colors. When the ship comes

Logistics will load them, flying
Them by crane dock to deck

While I follow over
The gangplank. Together, we'll cross

Rough waters to a country where
I put my cast-offs out of sight

And mind. What happened to my childhood
Schwinn hand-me-down

Decked with streamers and a thumb-bell? Don't
Consider what

I've put behind me. Beyond us, mountains
Keep themselves, and sky.

Fixing Antarctica

I keep taking the same photo over and over
As if to say Look, and Look. The light

Shifts minute by minute and everything
Holds: cormorant's flight, clouds
In motion, the glacier losing itself

Perpetually to sea, sea to sky—
And so we have returned, to consider what

Cannot be recovered. What is permanent
Is this moment, then this one, and always
Slipstreaming between them, the change.

Clock Erasure

Clocks thought ticking

Could bring death. Easy

Belief arose in the space

Uncertainty undermined. We

Like time, a fiction.

An erasure from "Does Anybody Really Know
What Time It Is?" by Howard Mansfield
NYT: March 10, 2011

Passage

"It was as if they had suddenly emerged into infinity."
Endurance, *Alfred Lansing*

Our ship carries fifty souls, no more,
Keeping bodies together over

Rollicking sea. Behind us all is light
And ice melting

Stone into vapor into air. We see the sun
But where is it? Ahead, water

Leaps to meet the sky, and you might wonder
Which hard grey would draw us

Farther into the cold. The astronomer
Says one thing, the sailor another

Who drives his hull over a surface
Looking on a day like this

As far as the eye can see hard as metal,
Uneasy as rock thrust upward by forces

His instruments fathom. Last night,
The first time in weeks, darkness fell

Across my porthole, and I knew I am
Traveling into winter. Having sailed for days

I'll fly from the longest day of the year
Over the equator's moonstruck

Flowers through flurries of twilight
And emerge body and soul

Shaking snow from my hair, into
The shortest day, asking the time.

WHILE I WAS AWAY

The dog didn't die.
My beloved, who unlike the dog
Feared I'd never come back

The same, is still here too,
Standing outside security
As if he might not know me or I him,

Holding a sign, my secret
Name. *Do you still?* Did I ever
Think he might not be? So much

To lose and the world changes
Everything. Though his whole head
Rises above the crowd

Even I can barely see
My slight self the window flashes
Brief reflection among

The other bodies, my head at average
Shoulder's level. How long has it been
Since I was only

So small? Tuft of something
Wafted his way in a drift of travelers
He stands against, solid, his eyes

Anxious then finding me at
Last and holding, his smile drawing
Me down the long hallway. He bends

And shoulders and arms fold like wings
Over me, around me, hold me
Beating against his heart.

GLASS HOUSE

At night, anyone hiding in the dark can see me
Fully illuminated. At the window, I

See only myself. I don't know why

I think of this now, during the light-
Brief day, while snow fills

The spaces between the oaks

And the trees open
Arms to light becoming

Weight in their embraces. Even a lucky life

Is heavy with grief. I pace my rooms
And each one changes

As I step into it. Outside, the house

Reflects upon the scene, the woods
I hide in. From there, I'm a flicker through snow-

Filled branches. Here, the room gives over

A whole wall to showing me
Everything I need to know.

Looking South

1. Habits of Invention

Here, in the face of the made,
Abandon me. In the dark

Where firelight licks
Stone walls, begin. I draw

My spear and take most
Careful aim. Draw the buck

The spear is looking for.
What if it's all

In my head. I can carry
The whole mountain there,

The striped cat stalking
My shadow. I know what

It feels like to share a skin,
Blood in my heart. Did I

Start with an idea of beauty
Or only end there? When

Weather turns and famine comes
It will be enough.

2. Rue

Maybe I needn't regret
Missed beauty. Opportunity never

Coming again. Things keep
Listing: Scott's hut, the good one

In the photos Charles sent
I can't stop looking at, all that

Evacuated light. The leopard
Seal who didn't find me

Delectable. Erebus's fired
Heart; ice caves' interior faces, hard

And blue to touch. Of course
The farthest point

I never reached. Go on:
Tell me it's an idea, no different

Than any other on the globe. Like them
It can be measured, crossed

Off the list. I could have
Pinned my flag right on it.

3. In the End

There is what we've seen
And what we've seen in photos,

Videos, between pages, in
Our heads. Sometimes it's hard

To distinguish one from the other, when I
Clearly remember lowering

Myself into the volcano, earth's
Center roiling so bright

I have to shield my eyes, an open heart
It wears on its sleeve, as if we lived

Still upon a star beating
Right there on the surface.

Last night I dreamed I slipped
My body down a cave

Lit within by its own blue
Shadow, satin I could barely

Shiver into. Who could
Paint those walls? When

Will I imagine I've seen
Enough? Always so much

Left, no matter
Where on earth we've been.

4. Looking South

My friend says he is All
About the Sublime Now. There he is

Open air, fancy-
Free, where light and ice

Add up to distance. This is possible
Exactly south of everywhere, in

A place ringed by nothing
But horizon on which every

Single point is equally
North, however things may look

From here, whatever any flattened
Map might suggest. Where I am

The world is gray, the world is
On schedule. I know, we're creeping

Back toward the light in the earth's
Own good time. But I

Remember what it was to be
All about. I would

Like to be again back in it, flighty,
Blown, unhinged, singing.

May Day

I sit as still as I can for as long as I can.

Outside, a cloud crosses the sun. Then another.

In April, a wild turkey took up temporary residence in the yard. The end of April. It had snowed again.

The bird scratched for acorns under the trees and dismantled the garden beds in search of grubs. She sat in one bed then and preened, lifting her feathers in outrageous circles like fans, every shade of brown its own flirtation. Then she found a patch of sun and went to sleep.

This was yesterday. I hoped she would build a nest in the high pines, but I had nothing to tempt her beyond acorns, grubs, the sunlight, a tin of seed.

I don't claim to be patient. I've been ready for winter to end, ready to end any chill I may have brought back with me. And yes, the snow has melted overnight, and I can see under it the foothills were always going green, the way they do every year, and soft, a green I can feel in the roof of my mouth like velvet, suddenly present.

Except where the cliffs take their stands against erosion, looking for the moment constant.

They cannot win. Even I can see, when I chance to be looking, how they shift, how they dust up and occasionally shake themselves off.

Self-Portrait as Erasure

1. It is, after all, just
What happens. Whether by time

Or light. By quirk or snowfall or the slow
Hand of wind over a surface: sand,

Water, even stone goes by. A feather
Flips over and flies. It is what

Happens to you, love, when I go
To sleep—and to me, I assume, when you

Sink to where we cannot keep
Each other, becoming as we do absent-

Minded. Waking to find you, I recall
What I must lose. Sometimes,

Talking, I look in your eyes and see
Every word vanishing. No

Matter. Let me tell you about that day
Chasing after humpbacks, our tiny

Boat fast-dancing in chop and wind, until
Alex killed the engine. We rose and fell,

Drifting on the swells. Chris, snap-snapping
His giant telephoto lens, shot a whale

Fluking in the distance, a whale
Bigger, closer, more focused, in every way

More present than our eyes
Could see. Later, over dinner, we looked

And looked. On video, what I got
Was not the whale's sudden surfacing

Right beside the boat, but its breathy
Spume, and, between me and it, Eddy

Doing his little jig of surprise. What I see
Now in my mind's eye: that fluke, lifted

And stilled forever against water
And snow, looming so close

We might touch it; Eddy letting his joy
Move him. I tell you, I can smell

The whale's sigh even now, its whoosh
Of fish and heat. Why hold on to whatever

Really happened, when
Memory writes over every bit.

2.

what happens
                                        surface

flies

sink as I do
                    what I must lose
vanishing

we chased
closer

                    look   what I got
little jig
mind's eye

move
        sigh
                hold on

SOME OTHER SUMMER

1. Last night while he slept, his brain rummaged
    Its bag of tricks and produced a flood,

    A traffic snarl, some place he had to get
    Beyond, though now he can't say what. Once,

    He was the one packing, me the one thinking
    I had things to see. Wherever he was, always

    He wished himself home. He would
    Sleep in his own bed every night if he could.

2. All spring and into our longest days, snow
    Kept piling up in the mountains, looming over

    The valley like a mind's weight. Now
    Relieved of its body, water rushes down

    The canyons, flooding creek-side houses,
    Soaking the fields until they reflect the sky,

    Unplantable. We can't believe
    It's mid-July, and still there's more snow

    Up there, deep and blue and breathing out
    Cold far below the glaciers and snowfields

That persist all summer.
                              Last night
While he was dreaming a sinkhole

Opened forty feet wide in the sodden earth
And forty deep, right under the highway. A girl,

Fifteen, lost to it. Her father at the wheel
Speeding to get home when everything fell

Away. In darkness, on either side, the lucky ones
Stopped and waited. Then turned back.

3. Meanwhile, already, the nights lengthen.
    Isn't this always happening? Crickets pipe up,

    Pipe up, invisible among the leaves,
    Waxing as they will into song

    With the waxing moon. Have you noticed?
    By August, they will be

    Overflowing the night. In the dark
    That carries us, in the dark we all carry

    Inside the future waits. Meanwhile,
    It keeps on coming.

Exit Interview

No plan could account for the moment
I woke into my first blizzard, or for

The ensuing habit of bliss. It didn't warn me
How I'd stand around waiting while

The wind dropped, the ship docked, my gut
Settled in. I can tell you what I remember

Wrong, how I planned one thing, did
Another. The map shows

The glacier flat, a white blob on a blue sea,
Also flat. Knowing the difference

Didn't prepare me for the glacier's face
Soaring out of the harbor and how it changes

Expression all day, shrugging
Itself off in great sheets, or how the sea

Rolls over and back and takes
Us with it. I didn't learn to leave

Myself behind. I didn't
Learn to stop inventing, at least

When reality stares me down. I send
My mind out front to look around

And when my body arrives everything
Changes. Changes again, the second

I'm looking back. Even now
Water thickens with shed ice, one floe

Large enough a leopard seal suns
Herself on it, content to wait until hunger

Draws a penguin close, another tender
Moment I couldn't plan for. When

The glacier shifts, growling, it too
Opens voraciously, invites me to look if

I'm dumb enough to get that close
Into its deep dream. I am plenty dumb-

Struck. I never expected the sunset
Would refuse to end long after I did.

Rumors of Topography

First, decide where water stops
And ice begins. Then, where ice

Ends and land takes over. As if

You will ever see the land, here,
Or anything lying under the ice

That cannot shrug it off. Try,

Beginning from the other end, to discern
Exactly the line between sky

And cloud, cloud

And mountain. Nobody's settled
Anything yet. Try to decide

Where the horizon locates itself

And whether the sun hovers above it
Or, selfless illusionist, has merely

Projected itself on the air: all

For your pleasure, that show of light
The moment darkness descends

And threatens not to lift. For months, also

For your pleasure, the question: Where
Darkness ends and you begin.

NOTES AND DEDICATIONS

Pages 17–19. "Proposal" is for Peter West of the National Science Foundation and for Cynthia Furse, engineer and Antarctic MacGyver.

Pages 21–23. The Belgian artist whose works are described in this poem is Francis Alys. These works and others can be seen at www. francisalys.com.

Page 26. "Self-Portrait is Not to Scale" is for Melanie Rae Thon.

Page 33. "Ship Songs" is for Jennifer Bogo.

Page 39. "Cold Heart" is for Andrew Farnsworth.

Pages 44–45. The John Burgess quote is from a conversation Burgess had with Errol Morris, as reported in Mr. Morris's *New York Times* Opinionator Blog, "The Ashtray: The Contest of Interpretation (Part 5)," on March 10, 2011.

Pages 46–47. "Charismatic Diatoms" is for Alex Culley and Chris Schvarcz.

Pages 52–53. "Inadvertent Self-Portrait" is for Pamela Balluck.

Page 56. *Stellar Axis*, on which this poem meditates, was an installation made at the South Pole in 2006 by Lita Albuquerque. It deployed 99 blue spheres of different sizes, which, on the summer solstice, aligned with 99 stars (invisible to the eye because of constant daylight) in the austral sky. Images can be seen at stellaraxis.com.

Page 61. "Cento from Various Non-Poetic Sources" is made with sentences from Ken Johnson's "Teaming with Transcendent Life" (*New York Times*, March 29, 2012); George Makari's "In the Arcadian Woods" (*New York Times*, April 16, 2012); John Noble Wilford's "Amazing Race to the Bottom of the World" (*New York Times*, December 12, 2011); Henry David Thoreau's journal (6 May 1854); and Elizabeth Ironside.

Page 62. "Peacock Dolphin" is for PQ and Nandi.

Pages 63–64. "To Alice, the Beast Appears" is for Alice Alpert.

Page 74. "Antimanifesto" is for Cynthia Furse.

Pages 77–79. "Problems of Description in the Language of Discovery" is based on conversations with mathematician Kenneth Golden, who studies the permeability of ice. The title is stolen wholesale from Gillian Beer's essay, "Problems of Description in the Language of Discovery."

Pages 80–82. "Dogs of Ice." After Amundsen beat Scott to the Pole (Scott and other members of his team having died in the attempt), he and his party were criticized by the British for, among other things, having not only relied on dogs but having killed and, rumor had it, eaten them along the way.

Pages 83–84. "Abandon" was written in response to Joseph Hoflehner's photographic series *Frozen History*. For this and many other poems, I owe a debt to Charles Hood, who called my attention to Hoflehner.

Page 96. "Glass House" is for Brendan Constantine.

Pages 97–102. "Looking South." The friend quoted in section 4 is Charles Hood.

Pages 109–110. "Exit Interview" is for Bob Farrell and Tracey Baldwin.

Pages 111–112. "Rumors of Topography" is titled with a phrase taken from Michael Ondaatje's *Running in the Family*.

BIOGRAPHICAL NOTE

Katharine Coles is the author of five collections of poems and two novels. In 2010, she traveled to Antarctica to write poems under the auspices of the National Science Foundation's Antarctic Artists and Writers Program; this book comprises poems from that project. Coles is the recipient of fellowships from the NEA and the John Simon Guggenheim Memorial Foundation. Her poems, essays, and stories have appeared in such journals as *The Paris Review*, *The Gettysburg Review*, *Poetry*, *North American Review*, *Southwest Review*, *DIAGRAM*, and *Ascent*, and have been translated into Italian, Dutch, and Chinese. She has contributed invited chapters to *Research Methods In Creative Writing* (Palgrave-Macmillan, UK, 2012) and *Teaching Creative Writing* (Continuum Books, UK, 2008). As the inaugural director of the Poetry Foundation's Harriet Monroe Poetry Institute, she edited and co-authored *Blueprints: Bringing Poetry to Communities* (University of Utah Press and The Poetry Foundation, 2011); co-authored *Poetry and New Media: A User's Guide*, for which she also directed the working group; and co-facilitated the production of *Best Practices in Fair Use for Poetry*, produced by the Institute in partnership with the Center for Social Media at the American University. She is a full professor of creative writing and literature at the University of Utah, where she founded and co-directs the Utah Symposium in Science and Literature.